PUBLISHED 2021 BY DAAWIEHBOOKS AND DREAMHAUZ PUBLICATIONS

Cover Design & Interior Layout / Formatting by: Quest Publications

Email: *questpublications@outlook.com*

FOR ADDITIONAL INFORMATION WRITE TO:

Boniface Darwieh-Keelson

DarwiehBooks and Publications

P.O. Box AF 657, Adenta-Accra,

Ghana, West Africa

OR Contact me on the following Cell Phones

001-233 244765586

001-233 244684802

My other contacts are Email:

amawaa@yahoo.com

evangelistboniface@ymail.com

bonifacekeelson@gmail.com

Social Media:

www.facebook.com/boniface.keelson

www.facebook.com/boniface.keelson

ALL RIGHTS RESERVED

All scripture quotations are from the King James Version of the Bible unless otherwise stated.

ISBN: 978-1-988439-29-7

TABLE OF CONTENT

Introduction .... *viii*

Chapter 1. FROM A BACKSTAGE TO THE FOREFRONT 1

Chapter 2. JEMIMAH 5

Chapter 3. KEZIAH 15

Chapter 4. KEREN-HAPPUCH 21

Chapter 5. A FATHER'S INHERITANCE 29

INTRODUCTION

He had also seven sons and three daughters. 14 And he called the name of the first, Jemima; and the name of the second, Kezia; and the name of the third, Kerenhappuch. 15 And in all the land were no women found so fair as the daughters of Job: and their father gave them inheritance among their brethren.—Job 42:13-15 KJV

Job was a man who went through a lot of challenges in life. His story is shared in the book of the Bible named after him—the book of Job.

Satan buffeted him greatly. His seven sons and three daughters died in one day. His business got destroyed and burnt by fire and other natural disasters. His health was greatly affected. He was afflicted with boils and other horrible skin diseases. His wife advised him to give up on God and he rebuked her for that wrong advice. His friends accused him of wrong doings, alleging that his sins had brought about all the afflictions on him. His brothers, sisters, and acquaintances neglected him. Nevertheless, Job kept his trust in God. At the end of the book, God came through for him and turned away all his pain and gave him a new beginning with double blessings for all that he lost.

After God had turned away the captivity of Job, He blessed him with seven sons and three daughters in place of the seven sons and daughters who died.

The three daughters of Job named Jemimah, Keziah and Keren-Happuch, became remarkable, outstanding, front liners, and were greatly loved and liked by their father. The factors that contributed to the uniqueness of these three daughters are hidden in their names. These factors are what I seek to unveil in this small book. I sincerely believe that if anyone gets hold on these factors, he or she shall move from the backstage to the forefront in life irrespective of the circumstances.

Enjoy Reading!
BONIFACE

THE DAUGHTERS OF JOB

Boniface Keelson

1

FROM A BACKSTAGE TO THE FOREFRONT

He had also seven sons and three daughters. 14 And he called the name of the first, Jemima; and the name of the second, Kezia; and the name of the third, Kerenhappuch. 15 And in all the land were no women found so fair as the daughters of Job: and their father gave them inheritance among their brethren.—Job 42:13-15 KJV

In chapter one of the book of Job, it was the sons who were in the forefront. They had a birthday party every year, and they invited their sisters to come and share with them, but in chapter 42, it was the daughters who were paraded at the forefront.

These daughters were not only beautiful, but they were also remarkable and outstanding in the community. They were loved and liked by their father Job and he gave them properties and inheritance on the land just as their brothers.

THEY WERE REMARKABLE

The three daughters of Job were extraordinary, exceptional, and impressive. The reality is that no one becomes remarkable in life by accident. Various factors account for one becoming remarkable in life. Obviously, the daughters of Job did not become remarkable by accident.

THEY WERE OUTSTANDING

The three daughters of Job were excellent, superb, and clearly noticeable in the community. Such qualities are not bought in any supper market. Certainly, some factors contributed to their attainment of these qualities.

THEY WERE AT THE FOREFRONT

The three daughters of Job played leading roles or were in positions of prominence. This is evident by the fact that their names were provided in the Bible, and also by the fact that a number of things were written about them. The same cannot be said of their seven brothers whom nothing was said about. Being in the forefront certainly demanded qualities which the daughters of Job exhibited.

THEY WERE LOVED AND LIKED

The three daughters of Job were exceptionally loved and liked by their father. That explains why their father gave them properties and inheritance among their brothers in an environment and society where only male children were given inheritance. There might have been a reason or reasons behind their father's exceptional love for these three daughters.

In a nutshell, the daughters of Job exhibited unique qualities that made them remarkable, outstanding, front liners, and loveable. Since such factors were not mentioned in the writings, we can only attempt to decode them from the beautiful and amazing names that Job gave to them.

2

JEMIMAH

He had also seven sons and three daughters. 14 And he called the name of the first, Jemima; and the name of the second, Kezia; and the name of the third, Kerenhappuch. 15 And in all the land were no women found so fair as the daughters of Job: and their father gave them inheritance among their brethren.—Job 42:13-15 KJV

THE DOVE

The name Jemimah stands for a dove and daylight. It would therefore be right to assume that by exhibiting the combined qualities of a dove and daylight, Jemimah became remarkable, outstanding, a front liner, and loved by the father. It can equally be deduced that anyone who exhibits the qualities of a dove and daylight will emerge a significant person in life just as Jemimah did.

QUALITIES OF THE DOVE

Without doubt there are bound to be countless symbolisms of the dove in this world. The few symbolisms of the dove I share with you in this chapter are not merely generalised ones but that which can be found in the word of God (the Bible).

1. A Dove Symbolizes Peace:

After 40 days of rain and destruction in the days of Noah (GEN 8:8-11), it was the dove that brought back news of hope and peace for the Earth. The quality of peace, which is depicted in being a peaceful person, a lover of peace, and being a peace maker will carry a person from the backstage into the forefront of life. Love peace and pursue it. As far as it is within your means, live at peace with all people and you shall endear yourself to others who will end up liking and loving you. Your peaceful nature, though may be taken for granted by others, will catapult you to greatness.

2. A Dove Symbolizes Faithfulness:

According to (GENESIS 8:6-12) Noah first sent out a raven to check and see if there was dry land but it returned no more. Perhaps it settled on some carcass and forgot about the fact that it had been sent (unfaithfulness). So, Noah sent out a dove and it came back because it had no where to perch. He sent it out the second and the third time. When it was sent out the second time, it came back with an olive branch in its beak. When it was sent out the third time it did not come back. Even though it never returned on the third assignment, it was an indication to Noah that it had found a new home and therefore the earth was thoroughly dried up. To have been sent repeatedly indicated faithfulness and reliability on the part of the dove. The virtue of faithfulness can carry anyone to the highest peak of prominence.

3. A Dove Symbolizes Cleanliness:

Doves display the virtue of cleanliness. That was why unlike the raven the dove sent out by Noah (GEN 8:8-11) would not even touch the ground if it were muddy and messy. The virtue of neatness and cleanliness will forever open doors of acceptance for those who exhibit them.

4. A Dove Symbolizes Purity:

Doves are naturally pure birds. The writer of Song of Solomon calls the dove an undefiled bird (SONG OF SOLOMON 5:2, 6:9). Though we live in an impure world, it is possible to live a pure life. My prayer for you is that like the dove, you will learn to keep a pure heart (MATT 5:8), pure thoughts (PROV 12:5), speak pure words (PSALM 12:6), keep your marriage pure (HEB 13:4), have pure eyes (SONG OF SOLOMON 1:15), keep your ways pure (PSALM 119:9), let your hands be clean (JAMES 4:8) and above all, always have pure motives (TITUS 1:15).

5. A Dove Symbolizes Wisdom:

Doves are wise. The prophet Jeremiah in admonishing the children of Israel concerning their impending danger asked them to act wisely like the dove. According to JER 48:28, the dove by wisdom makes its nest on the side of a hole or by the cleft of a rock, so that it may escape with the young ones into the rock for safety should a hawk or any dangerous predator pursue them. The writer of the book of Song of Solomon affirms this wisdom of the dove in Song of Solomon 2:14.

6. A Dove Symbolizes Spirituality:

Doves are known to symbolize spirituality. Among the animals God requested from Abraham in establishing a covenant with him was a dove (GEN 15:9). Doves were also used for the Levitical offerings (LEV 1:14). Joseph and Mary offered doves as their offering when they dedicated baby Jesus in the temple. Such burnt offerings were voluntary and represented surrender, devotion, and commitment to God. Absolute surrender, devotion, and commitment to God spiritually, will certainly project anyone above his or her contemporaries. Be spiritual and keep at it for life.

7. A Dove Symbolizes Harmlessness:

Doves are harmless birds. When our Lord Jesus warned us of the persecution that was to come because of believing in Him and preaching the gospel, He told us to be wise as serpents and harmless as doves (MATT 10:16). Being harmless connotes being simple, calm, innocent, and nonretaliatory. Any person with these rare qualities shall surely stand out one day.

8. A Dove Symbolizes the Holy Spirit:

Although this quality could not have been in Jemimah's life because they did not have the Holy Spirit at the time, I felt it would be helpful for me to add it because we are blessed with the Holy Spirit in our day.

At the baptism of our Lord Jesus Christ, the Bible records that the Holy Spirit descended upon Him in the style and form of a dove. It is important to note that the Holy Spirit is God and not a dove. The dove is just a symbol of how the Holy Spirit descended upon Jesus in baptism (MATT 3:16). Being filled with the Holy Spirit and being directed and influenced by the Holy Spirit is a key factor that would push any person from obscurity into the limelight. Do not play down on Apostle Paul's admonition to be filled with the Holy Spirit (Ephesians 5:18).

DAYLIGHT

Remember it has been aforementioned that the name Jemimah also means daylight. In this session we shall look at some qualities of daylight.

QUALITIES OF DAYLIGHT

May I share with you seven great symbols of daylight from the bible bearing in mind that there could be countless meaning of same in the bible and in other literature.

1. Daylight depicts The CLEARANCE of DARKNESS.

At creation, the first thing God did was to clear off all the darkness covering the face of the earth by calling forth light to appear (GEN 1:1-5). When God clears away all the darkness of obstruction from your path, you do not struggle to shine and to rise to significance in life.

2. Daylight depicts JOY.

The book of Psalms attests to that in Psalm 30:5 – weeping may endure for a night, but joy comes in the morning. Living a life of happiness and joy obviously put you ahead of many. Spread joy and happiness wherever you are. Learn to always express joy and contentment in your life and you will certainly be making a headway to greatness.

3. Daylight depicts WORK.

Our Lord Jesus made it point blank that we must do the work of God while there is daylight (JOHN 9:4). Daylight therefore depicts the hour of work. Hard work they say, does not kill. All who engage in work and do not lazy about are likely to rise to prominence. Hard work pays!

4. Daylight depicts GOOD CONDUCT.

We are admonished by God through the Apostle Paul to conduct ourselves as people of broad daylight, and not to indulge in revelry and drunkenness, nor in lust and debauchery, nor in quarrelling and jealousy (ROM 13:13). Good conduct is a rare virtue that will cause anyone to become a remarkable person in life. Do not trade your good conduct for worthless things, you will surely regret it.

5. Daylight depicts RIGHTEOUS DEEDS.

Jesus clearly stated that those who operate in the dark do so because their deeds are evil. But those who operate in the day have embraced the light of God and as a result they engage in deeds of righteousness (JOHN 3:19). Righteousness and righteous deeds are keys that open great doors of prominence. Mark the perfect man and behold the upright. The end of that man is peace (PSALM 37:37)

6. Daylight depicts HELP and SUPPORT.

King Saul sent a word to the people of Jabesh-Gilead that by the time the sun was hot the next day they would receive help (1 SAM 11:9). People who receive help are more likely to climb higher faster than their counterparts in life. May God send help through human agents into your life speedily. Another truth about help and support is that those who help and support others in life do not struggle to shine. I pray you do not fall short of the virtue of helping and supporting others.

7. Daylight depicts The SHINNING of GOD'S LIGHT.

The shinning of God's light on your destiny shall certainly cause you to shine and outshine in life. That is why the Prophet Isaiah is bold to announce that; Arise, shine; for your light is come, and the glory of the Lord is risen upon you (ISAIAH 60:1). Apostle Peter affirms Apostle Paul's teachings (2 COR 4:6) that as the day star of God (Jesus Christ the Light of the world) arises in a man's life (heart) all the darkness in his/her life and along his/her path gives way automatically (2 PETER 1:19). My prayer is that the glory of the Lord shall rise upon you. I pray that the day star shall arise strongly and brightly in your life and destiny.

3

KEZIAH

He had also seven sons and three daughters. 14 And he called the name of the first, Jemima; and the name of the second, Kezia; and the name of the third, Kerenhappuch. 15 And in all the land were no women found so fair as the daughters of Job: and their father gave them inheritance among their brethren.—Job 42:13-15 KJV

The name Keziah stands for fragrance, preciousness, and pleasantness. The name is derived from the flower plant cassia, known for its lovely fragrance. It was part of the spices used in making the precious anointing oil in the days of the Aaronic priesthood.

QUALITIES OF CASSIA

I may not know of all the symbolisms of the cassia plant. However, permit me to share the little I know about it from the Bible with you in this chapter.

1. Cassia connotes FINEST.

When instructing Moses in the book of Exodus to prepare the Aaronic anointing oil, God asked him to go for the finest spices of which cassia was mentioned (EXODUS 30:22-29). Finest implies something of excellent and admirable quality. Anyone who exhibits excellent and admirable qualities in life is bound to do well and go extremely far.

2. Cassia connotes PRECIOUSNESS.

We say something is precious when it is costly and highly priced or irreplaceable. In Psalm 133:2, the preciousness of the Aaronic Anointing is mentioned. Among the components used in making the Aaronic Anointing as afore mentioned include the cassia plant. That is why cassia connotes preciousness. Any person with qualities that are not easily replaceable turn out to be costly and highly priced in this life and certainly ends up on the seat of prominence. Like Keziah, I pray you exhibit such rare qualities in life.

3. Cassia connotes ENTERPRISING.

The cassia plant from which the name Keziah was derived was also used both as a commodity and a currency for merchandise according to Ezekiel 27:19. Having a cassia quality could then mean, being business minded and enterprising in life. All who are focused and enterprising in this life end up climbing the ladder of opulence.

4. Cassia connotes DEVOTION TO GOD.

An acacia wood which is of the cassia plant family from which the name Keziah was derived, was specifically used in making the holy altar of God in the days of Moses (EXODUS 30:1; EXODUS 38:1). Cassia therefore connotes devotion to God. This implies ardent affection towards God in yielding one's heart to Him with reverence, faith, and piety in every act, especially in personal fellowship, prayer and intimacy with His word. All who walk this path, end up beautifying their destiny on earth.

5. Cassia connotes FRAGRANCE.

In Psalm 45:8, the fragrance nature of cassia is portrayed, Cassia carries in it a sweet aroma. As children of God we are to carry in our nature the aroma of Christ and to spread same everywhere we go. In his second epistle to the Corinthians, Apostle Paul clearly stated that the believer is to spread forth the fragrance of Christ among fellow believers (2 COR 2:15-16). We do so by expressing godly joy, love, and the calmness of Christ wherever we go. Those who successfully do so, are easily loved and warmly received everywhere. As a result, they do not struggle to shine or become remarkable in life.

6. Cassia connotes the PRESENCE of GOD.

In making the Ark of the covenant, Moses was instructed by God to use acacia wood (EXODUS 25:10, EXODUS 26:15). The Ark of the Covenant was carried along with the children of Israel all through their wilderness journey. The main significance of the Ark of the Covenant was that it depicted the presence of God amid His people. The truth is that any person who has God's abiding presence in his or her life cannot be ignored or relegated to the backstage of life.

7. Cassia connotes RESISTANCE to DECAY.

Acacia was extremely strong and could resist all forms of decay (EXODUS 25:10). Insects and all agents of decay cannot overpower the acacia wood. It is difficult for water to penetrate an acacia wood. It can never be rotten and therefore can never produce bad or smelly odor. This significant but rare quality in the life of any individual will push him or her ahead in life. Our world is in dire need of persons who cannot be corrupted by worldlines, lust, pleasure, and earthly gains. Those who stand out, possessing this virtue shall end up on top in life.

8. Cassia connotes REFRESHING.

Like an air refresher in our day, the cassia plant had a sweet smell that refreshed its environment. Writing to the Corinthian church in his first epistle, Apostle Paul reminded them of how Brother Stephanas and his household has been extremely good in the work of God and how he refreshes believers everywhere he operates (1 COR 16:15-18). Those who refresh others are like the cassia plant which emits sweet fragrance and shall always emerge incredibly significant in life.

4

KEREN-HAPPUCH

He had also seven sons and three daughters. 14 And he called the name of the first, Jemima; and the name of the second, Kezia; and the name of the third, Kerenhappuch. 15 And in all the land were no women found so fair as the daughters of Job: and their father gave them inheritance among their brethren.—Job 42:13-15 KJV

HORN OF BEAUTY

The name Keren-Happuch means the Horn of Beauty. The horn of beauty in those days stood for a jar of eye paint. It was used by the women to highlight their eyes. It was a kind of cosmetic applied around a lady's eyes to enhance her beauty. The idea of the name Keren-Happuch therefore was that the girl was so naturally beautiful that she would not need to apply artificial cosmetics to enhance her beauty. The reality therefore was that this daughter of Job was endured with Pure Beauty. Thus, Keren-Happuch meant Pure Beauty.

QUALITIES OF PURE BEAUTY (HORN OF BEAUTY)

Permit me to share with you in this chapter eight undeniable qualities of Pure Beauty.

1. Pure Beauty is NATURAL.

Pure beauty does not need excessive enhancement with all manner of cosmetics and extensions. It is modest in its enhancement and naturally stands out. In his first epistle, Apostle Peter admonished ladies not to be excessive in trying to enhance their beauty (1 PETER 3:3). Indeed, true beauty is borne out of natural beauty and it is admirable. This quality obviously brought Job's third daughter Keren-Happuch into the limelight.

2. Pure Beauty is MODERATE and MODEST.

Those with the virtue of pure beauty are not over elaborate in their appearance and disposure. They are simple, moderate, modest, and yet elegant. That is what Apostle Paul in the early days of the church advocated for Christian ladies. The Apostle wrote: In like manner also, that women adorn themselves in modest apparel, with shamefacedness and sobriety; not with braided hair, or gold, or pearls, or costly array; But (which becometh women professing godliness) with good works (1 TIM 2:9-10). The Apostle was in no way asking women not to enhance their beauty with any of the afore mentioned elements. He only admonished that they be simple, modest, and moderate. That indeed is true and pure beauty, and it is admirable.

3. Pure Beauty is INNER BEAUTY.

Pure beauty is more of character than appearance and dress code. This is not to say dressing is to be taken for granted. Remember people will certainly judge you by your outward appearance before they consider your character. Nevertheless, no matter how elegant one's appearance might be, a slight flaw in character completely wipes off the gains of any elaborate appearance. That is why Apostle Peter would admonish that let true and pure beauty emanate from the inner man and not from elaborate and extravagant dressing (1 PET 3:3-4). The qualities of meekness, calmness, respect, courtesy, and gracefulness should be more desired and placed above outward adorning. Being gentle and lowly in heart like our Lord Jesus Christ (Matt 11:29) and possessing inner strength (EPH 3:16) are also necessary qualities of inner beauty. Those with such qualities like Keren-Happuch would forever be cherished and highly esteemed.

4. Pure Beauty is BEAUTY in the SPIRIT.

It is beauty without contamination or pollution of one's spirit. It is beauty with a sweet and delightful spirit. That is why the Prophet Malachi admonish couples to take heed of their spirits. Spouses are to take heed of their spirits and maintain it as sweet and beautiful as possible to enjoy their marriages (MAL 2:15b). Beauty in the spirit is enhanced when we have communion with God, feed on the word of God, get refreshed by the Holy Spirit, and maintain purity in our hearts. All who do that emerge in glory and rise to higher heights. Basic characteristics of beauty in the spirit are:

    Good Spirit -NEH 9:20
    Right Spirit – ROM 51:10
    Faithful Spirit – PROV 11:13
    Sweet Spirit – PSALM 32:2
    Contrite and Humble Spirit – ISAIAH 57:13
    Graceful Spirit – ZECH 12:10
    Quiet/Restful Spirit – 1 PETER 3:4

5. Pure Beauty is BEAUTY with BRIANS.

Beauty without brains is a bizarre combination. It is regrettable that many persons focus on personal appearance and elegance but are completely empty in their brains. Beauty is never complete without wisdom. That is why in beauty pageants there is always a segment to test the 'brains' of the contestants. Like Abigail, any person with good understanding (brains) and a beautiful countenance (1 SAM 25:3) will be cherished, loved, and would end up as a remarkable person in this life.

6. Pure Beauty is BEAUTY with HARD WORK.

Pure beauty is beauty with hard work and dedication. Like the Proverbs 31 woman, true and pure beauty is also a combination of hard work and beautiful countenance (PROV 31:10-29). The bible character that readily comes to mind anytime we think about beauty with hard work is the beautiful damsel called Ruth. She was prepared to soil her hands on farm work to bring food on the table for herself and her precious mother-in-law even though she was very pretty (RUTH 2:2-18). Beauty and laziness cannot be appreciated and takes people nowhere. A combination of beauty with hard work is always cherished dearly everywhere.

7. Pure Beauty is BEAUTY with THE FEAR OF GOD.

Anyone who has physical beauty but does not fear God is a strange beast yet to be revealed. Run away from all such persons. Satan is the master character of beauty without the fear of God. A person with beauty without the fear of God is considered a beauty with a beast inside, ready to show its true colours at the right time. Proverbs 31:30 says: favour is deceitful, and beauty is vain: but a woman that **FEARS** the Lord, she shall be praised. There cannot be true or pure beauty without the element of the fear of God.

THE DAUGHTERS OF JOB

5

A FATHER'S INHERITANCE

He had also seven sons and three daughters. 14 And he called the name of the first, Jemima; and the name of the second, Kezia; and the name of the third, Kerenhappuch. 15 And in all the land were no women found so fair as the daughters of Job: and their father gave them inheritance among their brethren.—Job 42:13-15 KJV

A FATHER'S INHERINTANCE

The last factor that most likely shot the three daughters of Job into the forefront was the fact that their father gave them inheritance among their brothers. An inheritance from a father could give you a giant leap in this life. Therefore, in this chapter, we shall take a brief look at a Father's Inheritance. We shall consider inheritances from a natural or biological father, a foster father, a boss father, a spiritual father, and the heavenly father.

1. INHERITANCE from a BIOLOGICAL FATHER

First, let us look at a father's inheritance from a biological father.

Property or Material Inheritance from a Biological Father.

In this account, Job the father gave to his three daughters property inheritance among their brothers. We read from Genesis 25:5-6 that Abraham gave all his properties to his biological and promised son Isaac. One notable inheritance you can get from a biological or natural father is property or material inheritance.

Training and Counselling Inheritance from a Biological Father.

The popular Proverbs 31 was a word of counsel given by a mother to her son who had just been made a king. King David on his death bed reminded his son of all the training he had received from him, admonished him with his last admonition, and charged him with some responsibilities (1 KINGS 2:1-4). A father's training and counsel is another great inheritance one can receive from a biological or natural father.

Prophetic and Spiritual Inheritance from a Biological Father.

A spiritual or prophetic blessing from a biological father could sometimes be more valuable than gold. Esau vowed to kill his brother Jacob because their father gave the best spiritual and prophetic blessings to Jacob instead of him (GENESIS 27:41). Jacob would not die until he had finished releasing prophetic and spiritual inheritance to his children (GENESIS 49). A biological or natural father may unleash prophetic or spiritual blessings as inheritance upon his child.

2. INHERITANCE from a FORSTER FATHER

One could likely inherit greatly from a foster father. A foster father is a person who functions in your life as a real father. Someone who took up responsibility over you in place of your natural or biological father.

Property and Material Inheritance from a Foster Father.

Abraham had a brother known as Haran who died and left behind a son called Lot (GENESIS 11:31). When God called Abraham to leave and go to the place He was to show him, Abraham carried along Lot (GEN 12) and took full care of him as a foster father. When God prospered Abraham in Genesis chapter 13, he settled Lot with some of his physical blessings and Lot became prosperous too (GENESIS 13:1-5). So, one can inherit property or material blessings from a foster father too.

Training and Counselling Inheritance from a Foster Father.

Abraham did not only give property inheritance to Lot, but he also gave him wise counsel (GEN 13:7-9), and training along with all whom he raised up as a foster father (GENESIS 14:14). Another foster father commonly mentioned in the Bible is Mordecai who raised up Esther his late uncle's daughter after the death of Esther's parents.

He blessed Esther greatly with life training, admonitions, and charges (ESTHER 2:5-7). Training, counselling, and life couching are among the best inheritance one may obtain from a foster father.

Prophetic and Spiritual Inheritance from a Foster Father.

Just as you can inherit a spiritual blessing from a natural father, you could also inherit great prophetic and spiritual blessings from a foster father. Jethro the father-in-law of Moses who became like a foster father to him in the land of Median prophetically and spiritually blessed him and gave him counsel at tough times of his ministry (EXODUS 4:18, EXODUS 18)

3. INHERITANCE from a BOSS FATHER

There is another father figure I call a Boss Father. A Boss Father is someone who fathers you in a trade, profession or calling. Such persons could also contribute to the significance of one's life just as natural fathers can.

Property and Material Inheritance from a Boss Father.

A Boss Father could give out property inheritance just like a natural father. I know of a mechanic whose master left him an entire workshop in his will because of his faithful service to him.

Training and imparting of skills are Inheritance one could receive from a Boss Father.

A Boss Father is also able to give quality training, counselling, and secrets to a faithful and obedient servant. If we must use the relationship between Moses and Joshua casually as a Boss-Son relationship, we could witness how Moses admonished Joshua three times in Joshua 1:6-9 to be strong and courageous anytime adversity visits. Certainly, a Boss Father could bless one by imparting skills, wisdom, and relevant tips for success and greatness.

Prophetic and Spiritual Inheritance from a Boss Father.

What most people do not know is that you can inherit a Spiritual Blessing from a Boss Father through faithful and obedience service under him or her.

4. INHERITANCE from a SPIRITUAL FATHER

Spiritual Fathers are significant figures in our lives through whom we access great inheritance in life.

Property or Material Inheritance from a Spiritual Father.

Just like natural fathers, spiritual fathers can also give physical inheritance like wealth, cars, properties, buildings, and even hand over entire churches to spiritual sons. However, the best inheritance spiritual fathers hand over to sons and daughters are not physical in nature.

The Teachings, Counselling, and Training of a Spiritual Father.

The greatest inheritance from a spiritual father is his wisdom and counselling. That is why God said He will give to us spiritual fathers (pastors) who shall feed us with knowledge and understanding (JER 3:15). Desiring breakthroughs through the ministry of a spiritual father without appreciating his wisdom is grievously unfortunate. The wisdom of a spiritual father comes to you through teaching, correction, rebuke (personal or general), training sessions, giving of orders and instructions (2 TIM 3:16, 2 TIM 4:2, TITUS 2:15).

You can enjoy the Grace of a Spiritual Father as an inheritance.

One great inheritance you can get from a Spiritual Father is that by virtue of your relationship and association with him, you could easily become a partaker of the very grace upon his life. Apostle Paul told the Philippians that because they were his spiritual children, they had been privileged to become partakers of the grace upon his life and ministry (PHIL 1:7). Those who know little about this, may downplay the relationship they have with such spiritual fathers, thinking they are of equal grace, only to hit the rock when left on their own.

You can enjoy the Anointing of a Spiritual Father as an inheritance.

Anointing is another great inheritance that can be transferred from a spiritual father to a spiritual. God asked Moses to assemble seventy of his spiritual sons before Him so that He God would take the anointing upon Moses's life and put same on his seventy spiritual sons (NUM

11:24-35). Elisha by closely following a spiritual father – Elijah, ended up with a double portion of the anointing that was upon Elijah (2 KINGS 2:9-15).

You can enjoy Spiritual Mantles from a Spiritual Father as an inheritance.

Spiritual Mantles carry a lot of spiritual weight and value. Such mantles include items used by and on spiritual fathers. Even those who crucified our Lord Jesus considered His garment a great spiritual mantle that they bargained for whilst He was on the cross (MATT 27:35). Certainly, whoever finally got the garment received a meaningless piece of cloth because they were not Jesus' spiritual sons. The mantle of Elijah that fell upon Elisha was a spiritual mantle from a spiritual father. The cloak (special coat he wore in his prayer closet), books, and parchments (pieces of personal bible notes he had jotted down) of Apostle Paul (2 TIM 4:13) were all mantles if they fell into the hands of any of his spiritual sons. When I was leaving the University of Ghana, a friend of mine begged of me to hand over a jacket I wore for midnight prayers throughout my days on campus as a spiritual mantle. Recently, Bishop Margaret Idahosa handed over the personal Bible of the late Archbishop Idahosa (with notes and markings) to Pastor Chris as a spiritual mantle at a given ceremony.

You can inherit a prophetic and spiritual blessing from a Spiritual Father.

Pastor Enoch Adeboye constantly talks about the prophetic prayer of Paa Akindayomi—his spiritual father upon his life on the day he announced to him that he would be taking over from him as the General Overseer. According to Pastor Adeboye, the prayer was so intense that it caused the foundations of a building to shake. Evangelist Reinhard Bonnke often spoke about the spiritual and prophetic blessing of the great Evangelist George Jeffreys upon him the night before George Jeffreys went into glory. Apostle Paul on two occasions reminded his son Timothy to fan to flame the gift of God that was released into his life by the laying on of hands by the Apostle and some spiritual fathers. (1 TIM 4:14, 2 TIM 1:6-7)

5. INHERITANCE from OUR FATHER in HEAVEN

The highest and greatest inheritance from a father is the inheritance from our Father in Heaven. I will quickly take you through just three kinds of inheritance you can enjoy from our Father in Heaven.

KOINONIA: Fellowship and Intimacy as an Inheritance from the Father in Heaven.

Fellowship with our Father in Heaven is the number one inheritance we access from Him. It was the very first inheritance Adam and Eve lost when they paid heed to the voice of the serpent (GEN 3:8-11). Apostle Paul's conclusion of the book of Corinthians is that, the grace of our Lord Jesus Christ, the love of God, and the fellowship of the Holy Spirit might be with us (2 COR 13:14). The root word for fellowship in the original manuscript is Koinonia. This Greek word implies deeper fellowship, association, and joint participation with and in God. Any man who deeply gets into real fellowship with God through the Holy Spirit inherits the presence of God and functions in the authority of the Almighty. This kind of deep intimacy with God to me, is the greatest and highest inheritance a child of God can inherit from the Father in Heaven. People who inherit such blessings from God can boldly say like Elijah, the God before whom I stand, there shall be no rain or dew (1 KINGS 17:1).

Spiritual Blessings and Heavenly gifts as inheritance from the Father in Heaven.

Next to Koinonia is Spiritual Blessings from our Father in Heaven. Apostle Paul was one man who always prayed for his sons and daughters to be blessed by spiritual blessings from Heaven (EPH 1:1-3). These heavenly blessings include being blessed with supernatural wisdom, revelation, and knowledge of God. It also includes having the eyes of your understanding enlightened, enjoying the riches of His glory, and being blessed with any kind of the gifts of the Holy Spirit (EPH 1:17-19, EPH 3:14-19, 1 COR 12:4-10). These blessings must be earnestly desired, prayed for and sought after all the days of our lives (1 COR 14:1).

Material and Physical Blessings as inheritance from the Father in Heaven.

I personally believe that the least of all the inheritance we may inherit from our Heavenly Father is Material Blessings. Though it is supposed to be the least and the easiest, the devil has somehow succeeded to make it appear as the paramount inheritance that believers of today seek after from the Father in Heaven. The components of material blessings from the Father in Heaven include His favour, breakthroughs, financial abundance, and all forms of open doors. These material inheritance from God are supposed to flow freely into our lives once we are in fellowship with God and operating under the canopy of His blessings. Proverbs 10:22 makes us to understand clearly that it is the blessing of the Lord that makes us rich, and it does so without struggle. Our Lord JESUS whilst on earth admonished us to seek the Kingdom of God and its righteousness first and all these blessings shall come upon us naturally from our Father in Heaven (MATT 6:33). Brethren, God can bless us with all material blessings if we would simply realign our priorities in pursuing Him.

ABOUT THE AUTHOR

BONIFACE DAAWIEH-KEELSON is an ordained minister of the Assemblies of God, Ghana as well as a credentialed minister with the Pentecostal Assemblies of Canada. He is a fire-brand preacher of the Gospel of Christ. Having been raised in the Lord through Scripture Union, Boniface is a very disciplined and faithful minister in the Kingdom.

He has been involved in the ministry of the Assemblies of God at a front role since his days in the university. He served as the Assemblies of God Campus Ministry President at the University of Ghana Legon in the year 1996-1997.

He is a trained minister from the Assemblies of God Theological Seminary in Ghana and the Assemblies of God Seminary in the United Kingdom.

He was commissioned an Evangelist with full ministerial rights in 2005 as an itinerant minister and a revivalist.

He established the prayer resort known as the Assemblies of God Retreat Centre [Fresh Grace Prayer Grounds] in the bushes of Brekumanso near Asamankese of the Eastern Region in Ghana.

He is currently a missionary of the Assemblies of God, Ghana to North America, and the Snr Pastor-in-charge of Lighthouse Assembly of God, Toronto, Canada.

He is married to an incredibly supportive and dynamic wife—Evelyn Ama Obenewaa Daawieh-Keelson, affectionately called Mama Evelyn by church members.

Boniface Daawieh-Keelson has won a few awards and Citations including the Global Award in Missionary Leadership (2010) from the Global Leadership Training, USA.

www.ingramcontent.com/pod-product-compliance
Lightning Source LLC
Chambersburg PA
CBHW072036060426
42449CB00010BA/2284